SandCastle™
Primeros Sonidos

I0878874

Toñis y Toño

Cathy Camarena, M.Ed., and Gloria B. Ruff, M.Ed.

Consulting Editors
Lourdes Flores-Hanson, M.S.E., and Gloria Rosso-White

ABDO Publishing Company

capstone®
www.capstoneclassroom.com

Credits
Curriculum Coordinator: Nancy Tuminelly
Cover and Interior Design and Production: Mighty Media
Child Photography: Steven Wewerka, Wewerka Photography
Photo Credits: AbleStock, Brand X Pictures, Comstock, Photodisc

ISBN 978-1-4966-0359-3 (paperback)

Printed in the United States of America in North Mankato, Minnesota.
012015 008756

SandCastle™ books are created by a professional team of educators, reading specialists, and content developers around five essential components that include phonemic awareness, phonics, vocabulary, text comprehension, and fluency. All books are written, reviewed, and leveled for guided and early intervention reading, and designed for use in shared, guided, and independent reading and writing activities to support a balanced approach to literacy instruction.

SandCastle Level: Beginning

Ññ

ABCChDEFGH

IJKLLlMNÑOP

QRSTUVWXYZ

abcchdefgh

ijklllmnñop

qrstuvwxyz

Toñis

Toño

piñata

muñeca

araña

piña

bañera

Aquí hay una  .

Aquí hay una  .

Mira la .

Aquí hay una .

Mira la .

Toñis tiene una piña.
La piña sabe bien.

Toño tiene una piñata.

La piñata es un toro.

La piñata es grande.

La piña está encima de la piñata.

¿Cuáles de estas cosas contienen ñ?

Más palabras que contienen ñ

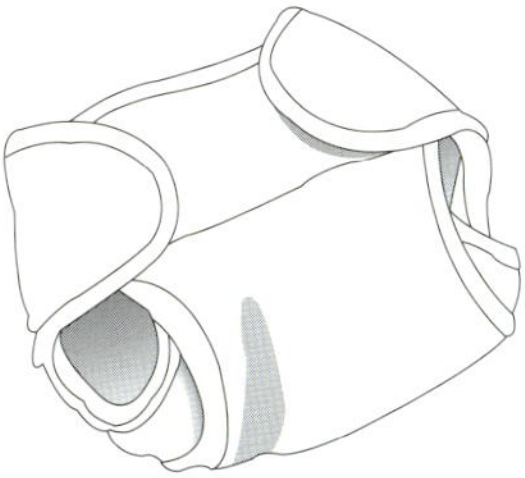

pañal

buñuelo

pañuelo

señal

leña

About SandCastle™

A professional team of educators, reading specialists, and content developers created the SandCastle™ series to support young readers as they develop reading skills and strategies and increase their general knowledge. The SandCastle™ series has four levels that correspond to early literacy development in young children. The levels are provided to help teachers and parents select the appropriate books for young readers.

Emerging Readers
(no flags)

Beginning Readers
(1 flag)

Transitional Readers
(2 flags)

Fluent Readers
(3 flags)

These levels are meant only as a guide. All levels are subject to change.

www.abdopub.com

www.capstoneclassroom.com